WHY I NEED JESUS

Who is God? What does that mean for me? Why should I care?

Contents

Chapter One

Why Do I Need Jesus?

Many people have been told that they need Jesus or they need to be saved. Have you ever wondered why you might need Jesus? Have you ever wondered what you might need to be saved from? Have you ever wondered why you should trust the Bible and the Christians pushing you to trust in Jesus? Have you ever wondered if you will be going to Hell? Have you ever wondered what the big deal is?

You may think that you are generally a good person and that life is going pretty well, so you don't need saving from anything. On the other hand, you might think you are a mess and have made so many mistakes that there is no way a perfect and powerful God would love you or save you. Maybe you'll look into Him after you get your life more in order. It is also possible that it sounds pretty good, but you've been told that science or history disproves the Bible, so it isn't trustworthy. You don't want to check your brain at the door.

Until you know who God is, why He is trustworthy, why faith in Him makes a difference, and from what you need saving, the Christian talk about Jesus may not make any sense at all. I'm hoping to answer some of these questions and hopefully help you to understand what all of the fuss is about.

1. **Chapter Review Questions:**

   a. Have you confessed your sins to God? Have you asked God's forgiveness? Have you received Jesus as Savior? (Romans 10:9)

   b. If not, what is holding you back? Do you believe you don't need saving? Do you believe you are too messed up to be forgiven? Do you think you need to do something first? Do you think God and/or the Bible has been disproved? Is it something else?

Chapter Two

What is Special about God/Jesus:

Questions about God/Jesus:

So you've probably heard Christians say that Jesus is God, and that He is holy, perfect, and all powerful. Maybe you've heard He is a big killjoy who tells you that you can't do the things that you think are fun. You've probably heard that God is love, but you see all the heartache in the world and wonder how an all-powerful, loving God could possibly allow all of that evil and heartache. You may have even thought that surely all of the hurt in the world proves that there can't be an all-powerful, loving God.

Are All gods Just One and the same?

The God of the Bible is not just another name for the god worshiped by other religions. Not all gods, worshiped by man, are the same. Many religions have a god who is kind of like a super hero. He or she has emotions and actions like a normal person, but has extra powers. This purported god is stronger and more powerful than a man. They may have special powers. They may live forever, but still they are just exaggerated people.

One example is the Greek and Roman Gods. They still have the same petty arguments that normal people have. They fight each other. They are selfish. They use people as little more than their pets. Why should we trust or worship a god or gods like that? Why should anyone worship a god that has so many faults and is so understandable?

There are also gods like Allah of the Muslim faith. Allah is a harsh god who requires everyone to live life exactly as he says. This includes destroying anyone who doesn't worship faithfully. His followers are rewarded for doing things like suicide bombing unbelievers. He treats women as possessions. If you read the Koran, the author doesn't seem to know whether to respect Jews or annihilate the Jews. In the beginning the Koran sounds almost like a Jewish sect, but by the end it is full of hate, destruction, and sexual abuse of women (rape of unbelievers, marriage to children, multiple wives, etc.). The self contradictions are almost schizophrenic.

If there truly is an all powerful creator God, wouldn't we expect that God to be so much beyond man that we cannot comprehend Him? Wouldn't we expect a God who is consistent in who He is and what He expects of His followers? Wouldn't we hope that He was loving and wanted what was best for us? All of this and more is true about the God of the Bible.

Creator God:

The first thing we should know about God is that He is the Creator of everything. The Bible starts with the verse *"In the beginning God created the heavens and the earth."* (Genesis 1:1) God spoke the very universe into existence. He created time and space, matter and energy, things seen and unseen. *"For by Him all things were created, both in the heavens and on earth, visible and invisible, whether thrones or dominions or rulers or authorities—all things have been created through Him and for Him."* (Colossians 1:16)

He didn't work hard to create everything that exists. It wasn't hard for Him to create all of the complexities of life or a perfect planet designed to support life or the vast expanse and beauty of the universe. God spoke everything into existence in 6 days. If you read Genesis 1 you will see Him repeatedly speaking things into existence. In fact it seems so easy for Him that Genesis 1:14-16 says on the 4th day that *"Then God said, 'Let there be lights in the expanse of the heavens to separate the day from the night, and let them be for signs and for seasons and for days and years; 15 and let them be for lights in the expanse of the heavens to give light on the earth'; and it was so. 16God made the two great lights, the greater light to govern the day, and the lesser light to govern the night; He made the stars also."* Creation was so easy for God that making all of the stars in the universe is stated almost as an aside, *"He made the stars also"*.

The wisdom, creativity, and power of the creator God is beyond anything we mortal men can comprehend. He is not a little god. He is an incomprehensibly awesome God.

He didn't just speak the universe, and everything in it, into existence. He is *"upholding all things by the word of His power"* (Hebrews 1:3a). The Bible also says, *"I know that, whatsoever God does, it shall be forever: nothing can be put to it, nor anything taken from it"* (Eccl 3:14). These verses basically state the most well proven law in all of science, the 1st law of thermodynamics which states that matter and energy cannot be created or destroyed. They can only change forms.

This is because God created all of the energy and matter in the universe and upholds it with His word. Nothing created can destroy what God has created. He is all powerful, omnipotent, omnipresent, and omniscient.

He also isn't limited by time or space. 2 Peter 3:8 states, *"But do not let this one fact escape your notice, beloved, that with the Lord one day is like a thousand years, and a thousand years like one day."* and Jeremiah 1:5 states,

> *"Before I formed you in*
> *the womb I knew you,*
> *And before you were*
> *born I consecrated you;*
> *I have appointed you a*
> *prophet to the nations."*

Basically, because God is outside time, He knows everything that has happened and everything that will happen through-out all of time. Because we are limited by time and space, it is hard to comprehend how someone could act outside of time, but what kind of God would deserve our trust and worship more than an incomprehensibly all powerful God who knows everything?

God of Love:

The God of the Bible is a God that is not only all powerful, but He is also a God of Love.

God made an Earth that is perfect for life. He gave us the sun, moon, and stars to give us light by day and by night, to give us beauty to look at, to help us tell time, to give us warmth, and to help things grow. He gave Abraham and Sarah a new home and a son in their old age. He protected the Israelites from starvation by putting Joseph in charge under Pharaoh in Egypt. He led the Israelites out of bondage in Egypt. He gave them laws to help them know what was best. Most of all, He sent His son to Earth to live a perfect life, to die a horrific death on the cross for our sins, and to rise again to life ascending to heaven.

When most people think of the sacrifices of Jesus, they think of Him being falsely accused, being beaten nearly to death, and dying an agonizing death on the cross. All of these were the ultimate sacrifice. It is more than any man or woman could ever comprehend willingly doing for another. Even if we wanted to do so for another, would any of us go through all of the way without tapping out? I don't think so.

For God, the sacrifice was so much more. As humans the mental and physical torment Jesus experienced is as great a torment as we can comprehend. Jesus did more. Jesus is an omniscient, omnipresent, omnipotent God. He is not limited by time or space or anything else other than His moral nature. Coming to Earth and living as a man is way more of a sacrifice than if one of us came down to Earth as a one celled bacteria. The limitations He put on Himself were unfathomably cruel. This takes claustrophobia to a whole new level. He gave up so much of what He was to come to Earth and live among us. *"Greater love has no one than this, that one lay down his life for his friends."* (John 15:13) Jesus sacrificed everything for us because He knew we could not pay the price ourselves. Jesus is love personified.

TRINITY: God the Father, God the Son, and God the Holy Spirit

Another incomprehensible thing about God is that He is a trinity: three in one. He is one God, but three persons: God the Father, God the Son (Jesus), and God the Holy Spirit. Our finite minds can't comprehend how someone can be three persons, but only one God. We have to accept that is what God is.

There are a number of analogies that help us understand the trinity, but none of them fully explain what the trinity is. We can not fully understand the trinity until the time we spend in eternity with Him, and although we will understand more in the afterlife, we may never fully understand.

One analogy of the trinity is the different roles of a person. I am a wife, a mother, and a business owner. I act differently acting in my different roles, but I have certain traits that are universal because I am me. As a wife I am encouraging, loving, submissive, romantic, and supportive. As a mom I am encouraging and loving, but I guide, teach, act as an example, and punish. As a business owner I encourage, train, discipline, and help my employees. You'll notice there are commonalities between my roles, but I also act differently in my different roles. The trinity is kind of like that, but they are more one and more three than my example. Although I sometimes talk to myself, I can't really interact socially with myself like the trinity can with the different parts of the trinity. I am more one. I can't truly be 3 persons.

The Trinity is also somewhat like the 3 states of water: ice, (liquid) water, and steam. They are all water. They are all H_2O, but if you look at ice, water, and steam, they all have different traits and don't look or act the same.

The last example I've heard came from a Southern Baptist pastor who has a food analogy for almost any Biblical principle. He always said that the trinity is as simple as cherry pie. If you have a cherry pie and cut it into three slices, when you look at it, it is clearly 3 different pieces of pie, but inside the cherry filling runs through the whole pie and is one cherry pie. There is no separation between the pieces. He would state, "the trinity is as simple as cherry pie."

If someone was making up a god to manipulate people, they would not make up something so confusing and incomprehensible about their god. On the other hand, a god who is the author of everything that exists is likely to have personal traits that are impossible for His creation to fully comprehend.

The trinity also is important in who God is. A loving God that is all alone would need His creation because He would be lonely and have no one to love. A trinitarian God has company and someone to love in the other two persons of the trinity. This God doesn't NEED His creation even if He wants and loves His creation.

Jesus: All Man and All God

Jesus is like no other. He is completely human, but He is also completely God. How this works is hard to understand for our limited human minds, but it is so. There are numerous events in His life that proves this truth.

First of all He was born of a virgin. *"18Now the birth of Jesus Christ was as follows: when His mother Mary had been betrothed to Joseph, before they came together she was found to be with child by the Holy Spirit."* (Matthew 1:18). Basically His mother was a young woman and His Father was God. Being of the blood of Mary, a descendant of Adam, allowed Him to be a kinsman redeemer for humanity, and being a descendant of King David made Him heir to the throne. Being born of the Holy Spirit made Him God (not that this was the beginning of His existence, but the beginning of His humanity).

Jesus then lived a perfect life. He never sinned once. He lived the life that we could not, both to be an example to us and to be worthy as the ultimate sacrifice for our sins. During His life He performed many miracles, such as turning water into wine, healing the deaf, the blind, and the lame, and even raising the dead back to life. No mere human could do these miracles, but the creator God could.

Then Jesus was convicted, by Jewish leaders, of blaspheme for claiming (truthfully) to be God. He was taunted, beaten, and nailed to a cross -- the most gruesome and painful death that the Romans had invented. While on the cross *"...Jesus had received the sour wine, He said, "It is finished!" And He bowed His head and gave up His spirit."* (John 19:30) This act strongly suggests He only died when He allowed Himself to die.

Willingly dying on the cross would have been an amazing act, but doesn't, in itself, prove He was God. The key proof of His Godhead is that three days after His death, He rose from the dead and was seen by many witnesses. "[1]The first account I composed, Theophilus, about all that Jesus began to do and teach, [2]until the day when He was taken up *to heaven,* after He had by the Holy Spirit given orders to the apostles whom He had chosen. [3]To these He also presented Himself alive after His suffering, by many convincing proofs, appearing to them over *a period of* forty days and speaking of the things concerning the kingdom of God." (Acts 1:1-3) Coming back to life proves all His statements and actions during His life.

Holy God:

God is a holy God.

"Be holy because I, the LORD your God, am holy"
(Leviticus 19:2).

What is holy? The Merriam-Webster dictionary definition states that holy is *"exalted or worthy of complete devotion as one perfect in goodness and righteousness."*

God's holiness is partly due to His absolute goodness. He never does anything wrong or mean or hurtful, but He does punish those who do wrong, mean, and hurtful things. He is so perfect that sinful man cannot stand to be in His presence. When God spoke to the Israelites on Mount Sinai it was necessary to keep everyone and everything off the mountain because they would be destroyed by His holiness. The people, in sight of the mountain, had to purify themselves and get right with God. The very presence of God was so awesome that the people stayed at a distance and even asked for Moses to talk to God and relay messages because being in God's holy presence was more than they could stand.

When Moses had been in the presence of God, his face would glow with such brightness that it terrified the people and he had to wear a veil.

When Moses asked to see God's glory (an amazing request considering all he had already seen), God responded *"I Myself will make all My goodness pass before you, and will proclaim the name of the Lord before you; and I will be gracious to whom I will be gracious, and will show compassion on whom I will show compassion." [20]But He said, "You cannot see My face, for no man can see Me and live!" [21]Then the Lord said, "Behold, there is a place by Me, and you shall stand there on the rock; [22]and it will come about, while My glory is passing by, that I will put you in the cleft of the rock and cover you with My hand until I have passed by. [23]Then I will take My hand away and you shall see My back, but My face shall not be seen."* (Exodus 33:19-23)   God's glory was so awesome that Moses couldn't look at God's face or he would die.

In Isaiah chapter 6, Isaiah is brought into the presence of God to have prophecy shared with him:

"[1]In the year of King Uzziah's death I saw the Lord sitting on a throne, lofty and exalted, with the train of His robe filling the temple. [2]Seraphim stood above Him, each having six wings: with two he covered his face, and with two he covered his

feet, and with two he flew. ³And one called out to
another and said,
'Holy, Holy, Holy, is the Lord of hosts,
The whole earth is full of His glory.'
⁴And the foundations of the thresholds trembled at
the voice of Him who called out,
while the temple was filling with smoke. ⁵Then I
said,
"Woe is me, for I am ruined!
Because I am a man of unclean lips,
And I live among a people of unclean lips;
For my eyes have seen the King, the Lord of hosts."
⁶Then one of the seraphim flew to me with a burn-
ing coal in his hand, which he had taken from
the altar with tongs. ⁷He touched my mouth with
it and said, "Behold, this has touched your lips;
and your iniquity is taken away and your sin is
forgiven."(Isaiah 6:1-7)

Notice how Isaiah is distraught at being in God's presence.
Being in God's presence helps him to see how sinful and un-
worthy he truly is. Nothing but God's grace can save him from
his sinful nature.

We truly cannot comprehend the God of the Bible. He is

greater and more holy and more worthy of worship than we can ever understand, but those of us who have trusted Him as savior are joyed to spend all of eternity trying.

As a holy God, the God of the Bible cannot stand to be around sin/evil. In the days of Noah God said in Genesis 6:5 *"Then the Lord saw that the wickedness of man was great on the earth, and that every intent of the thoughts of his heart was only evil continually."* The God of the bible could not abide the evil of the world and chose to destroy that evil by destroying every living thing on the Earth. Being a loving and merciful God, though, He saved Noah, his wife, his three sons, and their wives, and saved at least a pair of every animal kind on the Earth.

"The LORD has established His throne in heaven,
and His kingdom rules over all" (Psalm 103:19)

Judgment and the Wrath of God:

Most people don't like to think about the wrath of God. It is much more comfortable to think about a warm and fuzzy, loving God. Somehow wrath seems below God because with people wrath is frequently associated with a loss of self-control or wounded pride or a bad temper or selfishness. This couldn't be farther from the truth regarding the wrath of God.

As we previously read, God is a holy God. He hates evil. He can't abide theft, lies, impurity, hate, envy, disrespect, etc. A holy God would not be holy if He ignored evil. A holy God can only be holy if He judges objective moral evil. He is a righteous, perfect judge, unlike imperfect, human judges here on Earth. He perfectly judges evil. Because He is all knowing, He knows the whole truth and every bit of the truth. He even knows every thought we have or ever will have. Because He is holy, He gives perfectly just sentences to the guilty. Unfortunately, this does not bode well for the sinner and we all have sinned. God's wrath is the perfect administration of justice.

"2A jealous and avenging God is the Lord;
The Lord is avenging and wrathful.
The Lord takes vengeance on His adversaries,
And He reserves wrath for His enemies.
3The Lord is slow to anger and great in power,
And the Lord will by no means leave the guilty
unpunished.
In whirlwind and storm is His way,
And clouds are the dust beneath His feet.
4He rebukes the sea and makes it dry;

He dries up all the rivers.

Bashan and Carmel wither;

The blossoms of Lebanon wither.

⁵Mountains quake because of Him

And the hills dissolve;

Indeed the earth is upheaved by His presence,

The world and all the inhabitants in it.

⁶Who can stand before His indignation?

Who can endure the burning of His anger?

His wrath is poured out like fire

And the rocks are broken up by Him.

⁷The Lord is good,

A stronghold in the day of trouble,

And He knows those who take refuge in Him.

⁸But with an overflowing flood

He will make a complete end of its site,

And will pursue His enemies into darkness

(Nahum 1:2-8)

We do not want to be on the judgment end of our holy God's wrath. We desperately need to be under His grace.

Right and Wrong are defined by the creator God:

As Creator, God has the right to define right and wrong, what we should and should not do, and what we are and should be. *"Sovereign Lord, you made the heavens and the earth and the sea, and everything in them"* (Acts 4:24).

We were made with a purpose, primarily to serve and worship Him. Some may say, "why do we have to do what He wants?", but as the Creator, He has the right to say what His creation must do.

> *"18 So then He has mercy on whom He desires, and He hardens whom He desires. 19 You will say to me then, "Why does He still find fault? For who resists His will?" 20 On the contrary, who are you, O man, who answers back to God? The thing molded will not say to the molder, "Why did you make me like this," will it? 21 Or does not the potter have a right over the clay, to make from the same lump one vessel for honorable use and another for common use? 22 What if God, although willing to demonstrate His wrath and to make His power known, endured*

with much patience vessels of wrath prepared for destruction? [23] And He did so to make known the riches of His glory upon vessels of mercy, which He prepared beforehand for glory, [24] even us, whom He also called, not from among Jews only, but also from among Gentiles." (Romans 9:18-23)

The Creator has a full right to require whatever He desires from His creation. When we fulfill our purpose we find joy and peace because we are doing what we were created to do. When we live other than according to God's purpose, we feel anxious; we search for something to fill that hole in our soul; we feel loss; and we get caught up in lots of things that are not good for us in our search for pleasure and for meaning in our life. When we fail to live according to our purpose, we are also opposing the all powerful, holy God. We become the object of His judgment.

Below are a few more verses on God's sovereignty. It may be hard for us to submit, but that is what we must do as created beings of our Lord and Creator.

"Yours, LORD, is the greatness and the power and the glory and the majesty and the splendor, for everything in heaven and earth is yours.

Yours, LORD, is the kingdom; you are exalted as head over all" (1 Chronicles 29:11).

"Sovereign Lord, you made the heavens and the earth and the sea, and everything in them" (Acts 4:24).

"God disciplines us for our good, in order that we may share in His holiness" (Hebrews 12:10)

"'For my thoughts are not your thoughts, neither are your ways my ways,' declares the LORD. 'As the heavens are higher than the earth, so are my ways higher than your ways and my thoughts than your thoughts'" (Isaiah 55:8-9)

Chapter Review Questions:

1. Why and How is the God of the Bible different than other gods? (Psalm 104) (Psalm 18:30-50)

2. Why does it matter that God is the Creator of every-

thing? (Isaiah 45:9-23) (Jeremiah 18:1-12)

3. Do you tend to think more about God's love (1 John 4:7-17) or judgment? (Psalm 7:11) (Romans 2:5-11) Why is a proper balance important?

4. What does the trinitarian (3 in 1) nature of God tell us about His nature and character? (Genesis 1:26-30 *[pay attention to pronouns]*) (1 Peter 1:1-9)

5. What is holiness? (Psalm 99) Why is it important to understand God's holiness? (1 Peter 1:14-21) Do I have a proper view of God's holiness? (2 Thessalonians 1:5-10)

6. What does God's holiness have to do with His judgment and wrath? (Romans 1:18-23) (Hosea 11:8-11) Why is this important to understand? (Psalm 7:10-11)

7. How is God's wrath different than a normal person's wrath? (Romans 12:14-21) (James 1:19-21)

8. Why does God get to define right and wrong? (Romans 9:20-21) How does a proper perspective on this help us to submit and repent willfully and joyfully?

9. How does a proper view of God lead us to salvation?

Chapter Three

What About Me? Why do I need Saving and From What?

The Good, The Bad, and the Ugly

The Good:

You might wonder what such an incomprehensible, all-powerful God might possibly want with man.

> "⁴What is man that You take thought of him,
> And the son of man that You care for him?
> ⁵Yet You have made him a little lower than God,
> And You crown him with glory and majesty!

> ^{6}You make him to rule over the works of Your hands;
> You have put all things under his feet," (Psalm 8:4-6)

On the six days of creation, God made a lot of marvelous things, but He made humans special. The creation of man was more personal. The other things in creation were spoken into existence, but God breathed life into man. "Then the Lord God formed man of dust from the ground, and breathed into his nostrils the breath of life; and man became a living being." (Genesis 2:7) God's creation of man was different than His creation of other parts of the universe including other living creatures.

"^{3}Then God said, "Let there be light"; and there was light" (Genesis 1:3) Notice God spoke light into existence

"^{11}Then God said, "Let the earth sprout vegetation, plants yielding seed, and fruit trees on the earth bearing fruit after their kind" (Genesis 1:11) Even though plants are life, God spoke plants into existence.

"^{24}Then God said, "Let the earth bring forth living creatures after their kind:" (Genesis 1:24a) Even the land animals were spoken into existence generically.

"⁷Then the Lord God formed man of dust from the ground, and breathed into his nostrils the breath of life; and man became a living being." (Genesis 2:7) Man's creation was different. It was more personal. He didn't speak humanity into existence. He personally formed Adam, in particular, and "breathed into his nostrils the breath of life." Pay close attention to how much more loving and caring Adam's creation was compared to everything else.

"but for Adam there was not found a helper suitable for him. ²¹So the Lord God caused a deep sleep to fall upon the man, and he slept; then He took one of his ribs and closed up the flesh at that place. ²²The Lord God fashioned into a woman the rib which He had taken from the man, and brought her to the man" (Genesis 2:20b-22) God saw a need in Adam and then He personally fashioned a woman, a helper for Adam. The whole creation of humanity was personal. It was about particular people. It was face to face and based on personal touch. God showed He cared. He showed why He created the universe. He created it for mankind.

God also made man in His image.

"²⁶Then God said, "Let Us make man in Our image, according to Our likeness; and let them rule over the fish of the sea and over the birds of the sky and over the cattle and over all the earth, and over every creeping thing that creeps on the earth." ²⁷God created man in His own image, in the image of God He created him; male and female He created them. ²⁸God blessed them; and God said to them, "Be fruitful and multiply, and fill the earth, and subdue it; and rule over the fish of the sea and over the birds of the sky and over every living thing that moves on the earth." (Genesis 1:26-28)

Being made in the image of the all knowing, all powerful God gives us value, great value. We are not pond scum; we are made in the image of the creator God. This should change our view of ourselves and others. Human life is precious.

In addition, man was made to interact with God and was given certain attributes of God. The creation of man was made for personal interaction. God would provide for man like a Father takes care of his children. Man would worship God as is reasonable for His creation to do.

God also made man to rule over His creation and to take care of His creation. He gave us a position of honor. He gave us everything we needed, but also gave us responsibility and a purpose. Lastly, He gave us a choice. Would we honor our creator with our words and actions? Would we obey His commands? Would we take proper care of His creation? Sadly, the answer is "No, no, and no."

The Bad:

In the Garden of Eden, the paradise prepared for us by God, there was only one law: "[16]The Lord God commanded the man, saying, "From any tree of the garden you may eat freely; [17]but from the tree of the knowledge of good and evil you shall not eat, for in the day that you eat from it you will surely die." (Genesis 2:16-17). It wasn't very difficult. Adam and Eve (the first man and woman created) were able to eat anything they wanted and do anything they wanted. The only thing they were not allowed to do was to eat from the Tree of the Knowledge of Good and Evil. How hard could it be to obey a single law? Doesn't that seem so much easier than all of the rules and laws we are supposed to obey in society today?

The Bible isn't clear on exactly how long it took Adam and Eve to break the one and only law set upon them in the paradise

God had prepared for them, but context suggests it wasn't very long. This single bad decision by both Adam and Eve damaged God's perfect creation and we are dealing with the consequences to this day.

You may be thinking that is true of Adam and Eve, but that you didn't break this law. That isn't you, but have you ever lied, stolen something, been mean to someone, been selfish, or disrespected the God and creator of the universe? **"for all have sinned and fall short of the glory of God,"** (Romans 3:23). All of us have sinned and justly deserve punishment. If we had done nothing wrong other than deny our God and creator, we would be worthy of death.

Also, the very act of the first people, Adam and Eve, created in us a sin nature that has been passed down from generation to generation. Even when we work hard to overcome that sin nature, we will never be successful if we try to do it in our own power. We don't have the strength, self control, or righteousness to succeed by our own power.

The Ugly:

I'll say it again because it is so important, "If we had never done anything wrong other than deny our God and creator, we would be worthy of death."

"You too have done evil, even more than by our forefathers: for behold you are each one walking according to the stubbornness of his own evil heart without listening to me." (Jeremiah 16:12) More than any particular sin, it is ignoring God, disobeying God, and acting as if you get to chose what is good and bad, that is the ultimate sin.

If we read the Bible, it is full of God's holy judgment, not in wild anger, but in just holiness. The pre-flood era was judged because "... every intent of the thoughts of his heart was only *evil continually*." (Genesis 6:5) We see Egypt being judged with many plagues, including the death of every first born son of man and animal, for disobeying God's command to let His people go. (Exodus 6-12) We see Sodom and Gomorah being destroyed by raining down fire and brimstone (sulfur) for sexual and other sins. (Genesis 19) We see God even punishing His chosen people, Israel. They are punished for unfaithfulness including being sent off, out of their land, taken captive more than once. Should we expect anything different?

Many people think that a loving God wouldn't punish us because there are other people that are much worse, but we must remember other people are not the measuring stick by which we are measured. We are measured by God's word. We are measured in comparison to the perfect life of Jesus Christ. We might be an inch better than the thief, murderer, or rapist, but we are many light years worse than Jesus Christ. Any goodness in ourselves is so small in comparison to Jesus, that it might as well not exist. We only think we are good when we compare ourselves to the wrong reference — other sinful people.

Until we judge ourselves by God's word (The Bible) and by the life of Jesus, we can't see ourselves rightly. "There is a way that appears to be right, but in the end it leads to death." (Proverbs 14:12)

When God created man, He made us to fellowship with Him and to worship Him. Our true happiness comes when we do what we were created to do. When we are separated from God, we will never truly be happy or at peace. Sin is what separates us from God. "But your iniquities have separated you from your God; your sins have hidden His face from you, so that He will not hear." (Isaiah 59:2)

As long as sin separates us from God, we will ultimately get what we deserve, which is death. "For the wages of sin is death, but the gift of God is eternal life in Christ Jesus our Lord." (Romans 6:23) Luckily there is a solution to our problem, but before I go into the solution I want to share a few more things that might help you to accept God's truth and

God's salvation. I don't want you to dismiss it out of hand due to a belief that the Bible has been disproved.

Chapter Review Questions:

1. Why is a proper view of the creation of mankind important for understanding our relationship to God? To the environment? To other people? (Genesis 1:26-31, 2:15-25)

2. How does understanding the fall of man (Adam and Eve's choice to disobey God) help us to understand evil in the world? Evil in others? Evil in ourselves? (Genesis 3:1-21)

3. Have you sinned against your creator God? Do you understand what that means for your life and the afterlife? (Romans 6:23)

4. Is there anything you can do about your sin? (Romans 10:9)

Chapter Four

Why should I trust the Bible? Hasn't It Been Disproven?

Has the Bible been Disproven?

There are lots of very smart people who have declared with conviction that the Bible has been proven untrue. Unfortunately the motives of these people have to be questioned. They say they have disproven the Bible, but they use an axiom (assumed principle) that everything happens naturally and that supernatural things can't be true. If this is your axiom, then logically God can't be true, but unfortunately they never prove the axiom.

Many of these intelligent scientists are so proud of their intelligence that they can't stand to admit that there is an all powerful and all knowing God who makes them look small and unimportant. They don't like admitting that there is someone to whom they must answer. They want to consider themselves gods. This colors all of their studies and all of their conclusions. They are far from unbiased. In reality they are part of a religion of naturalism, a religion that makes man a god, a religion that puts denial of an all powerful, holy God as their highest tenant. Anyone who contradicts that tenant must be treated as an apostate. This is a big reason why pro-God, young Earth, global flood evidence will never be allowed in a secular, peer-reviewed journal.

Experimental Science vs Historical Science/Forensic Science

Before going into specifics, I need to explain the difference between experimental science, which is what most people think of when we talk about science, and historical or forensic science. Experimental science is following the Scientific Method.

1. Make an observation

2. Develop a Hypothesis

3. Conduct an experiment to test your hypothesis (must be the kind of experiment that can also disprove your hypothesis)

4. Draw conclusions from the results of the experiment. Does it support or negate your hypothesis? Are there other conditions that the experiment didn't test that need to be tested? Can you and others reproduce your results?

5. Repeat with a modified hypothesis and/or modified experiment.

Experimental science requires many experiments to even reach the point of being referred to as a theory. It requires a massive amount of experiments by many people over a large amount of time for anything to be considered a scientific law, but even then it may not be the complete truth. Newtonian physics was considered to be scientific law until Einstein proved Relativistic Physics. Newtonian physics worked well to explain things under normal conditions, but Einstein proved that it did not fully explain how the universe works because motion and time work differently when moving near the speed of light.

No science is ever truly proven. There are so many examples of "proven science" that have either been disproven, ie. an

Earth centric solar system proven to be Sun centric, or proven incomplete, like the Newtonian Physics vs Relativistic Physics. Anyone who says the science is proven doesn't understand science or is lying to you.

When you are trying to figure out what happened in the past, there isn't an experiment that will prove what happened. There are experiments that can prove what might have happened based on the evidence remaining, but nothing proves what did happen. Therefore, when forensically studying the evidence of past events, like the beginning of the universe, we can only look at clues to see if our theory matches the evidence or contradicts the evidence, and whether our theory correctly predicts new evidence that is subsequently found. Still we will never be able to prove 100% what is the truth. The only way to be 100% certain of what happened in the past is to be told by a trustworthy witness.

When different assumptions are made, different conclusions come from the same evidence. If we want to know how the universe and everything in it were made, we have to listen to the only witness, God.

I do understand that some witnesses are more reliable than others. If you know that a witness is honest, observant, intelligent, and has a good memory, you will be more likely to trust that witness than a witness who is known to lie or is known to not pay attention to details or is forgetful or is biased. Looking at evidence, we can see if the witness is most likely telling the truth or is more likely to be lying or mistaken.

I trust God's witness 100%, but if you don't, let us look at the evidence to see if God's witness or the theories of fallible men seem to match the evidence better.

Hasn't Carbon-14 (or Radiometric) Dating Proven an Old Earth?

The basic answer is "No", but let me explain radiometric dating and carbon-14 dating, so you can understand it and its limitations.

There are multiple kinds of radiometric dating methods, but all have a basic premise and procedure. It starts with a radioactive parent element that breaks down into a non-radioactive daughter element. There are 4 assumptions that are made in order to calculate the age from the measurements of how much parent and daughter elements are in a sample.

- Starting Condition: They assume how much parent isotope and how much daughter isotope was in the sample originally. (In many cases they assume the starting sample was 100% the parent isotope. This is not the case for C-14 dating as will be explained below)

- Constant Known Decay Rate: They assume that the parent isotope converts to the daughter isotope at a constant, known rate under all circumstances.

- Closed System: The assumption is that no parent or daughter isotope enters or leaves the sample. It is assumed that all parent isotope was there in the beginning and all daughter isotope came from the decay of the parent isotope, reducing the amount of parent isotope.

- Sufficient Decay: There needs to be enough time that a measurable amount of parent isotope has decayed into the daughter isotope.

Based on these assumptions, an age calculation can be made. The question we need to ask is "Can we trust these assumptions?"

When we are trying to figure out the unknown age of a sample, how are we supposed to know the starting condition of that long-ago date? There is no way to know how much parent vs daughter isotope was in the original sample. There is a high likelihood of error in this assumption which can massively change the calculated date.

Can we assume the system is closed and that no parent or daughter isotope entered or left the sample over the hundreds to billions of years the sample supposedly existed? Definitely not! Most of the isotopes are water soluble. Over multiple years it is inconceivable that water would not wash one or both isotopes into or out of the sample. Once again, this can massively change the calculated date.

Can we know the decay rate of the parent isotope? This is the only assumption that seems reasonable, but we still can't know if it is accurate, because nobody was there in the past. There is also evidence that rates were different in the past. Most radiometric decay is the parent isotope giving up 2 protons (beta decay), which is effectively a helium nucleus. Looking at zircons in granite, they can see damage to the crystal for each helium nucleus released and can test how much helium still exists in the zircon. There are known diffusion rates of helium in the zircons at different temperatures. If the decay rate was as slow as is believed, most of the helium should have diffused out of the zircons, but most of it is still in the zircons. This suggests the decay rate was faster in the past (during the flood?).[1]

With all of these problems with radiometric dating, we should ask, "How accurate is dating for rocks of known dates?" The answer is "not very accurate."[2]

Rock Formation	Known Age	Measured/Calculated Age
Hualapai Basalt	200 years	1,600,000 years
Kilauea Basalt	40 years	8,500,000 years
Mt Etna	37 years	700,000 years

Many people think that carbon-14 dating proves an old Earth, but carbon-14 has a relatively fast decay rate and measurable carbon-14 is gone in less than 100,000 years and isn't very accurate for more than around 4,000 years. It is also only used to date things that were once living because it is based on regular consumption of carbon, including carbon-14.

---

1. For more information see https://www.icr.org/article/helium-retention-zi rcons-demonstrates-young-earth . There are also secular sources suggesting the decay rate is not necessarily constant such as https://www.purdue.edu/ newsroom/research/2010/100830FischbachJenkinsDec.html and https:// arxiv.org/pdf/2012.00153.pdf . All of this suggests this assumption can not be counted on.

2. See <u>The Global Flood: Unlocking Earth's Geological History</u> by John D. Morris pg 138

Solar radiation strikes the nitrogen in the atmosphere and converts a small percentage from nitrogen-14 to carbon-14. This carbon-14 then decays into carbon-12. It is assumed that all living creatures take in carbon in the same proportion as the atmosphere and that the atmosphere has always had the same proportions of carbon-14 and carbon-12. Plants use carbon dioxide (CO_2) to make sugars and other organic compounds that have the same ratio of the carbon isotopes in these molecules as is in the atmosphere. Herbivores then eat the plants getting the same proportion of carbon isotopes. Carnivores then get the same proportion of carbon isotopes from eating the herbivores. When the plant or animal dies, it quits taking in carbon and the carbon-14 decays into carbon-12.

The question is, "Are these assumptions correct?" The Earth's magnetic field, which protects the Earth from solar radiation, has been halving approximately every 1400 years. A higher magnetic field in the past would mean a lower proportion of carbon-14 in the atmosphere and in living creatures in the past because the magnetic field would block more of the solar radiation reducing the amount of carbon-14 in the atmosphere. Having a lower proportion of starting carbon-14 causes the calculated age to be older than it really is.

An example of false assumptions causing dating errors is as follows. Skeleton's were found in Repton, England and carbon-14 dated to have died in the AD 600s-700s. The only recorded large deaths were of a Viking army in AD 873-874. The researchers thought there must have been two Viking invasions and only one was recorded. What is the truth? Vikings eat mostly fish and other sea creatures. These creatures are much farther down the food chain and have a lower proportion of carbon-14 in them. Because the starting proportion of carbon-14 was lower, the age calculations were off and said the skeletons were older than they really were. The researchers should have trusted the eye-witnesses.[3]

There are many other problems with carbon-14 dating.[4] Besides all of these problems, carbon-14 can't be used to date rocks and therefore can't be used to date the Earth.

Is the Earth really Billions of Years Old?

Many of us have been told that the Earth and the Universe were created billions of years ago by the Big Bang. Unfortunately for the supporters of the Big Bang Theory, it doesn't match the data very well and its predictions keep failing, unlike

---

3. See https://www.icr.org/article/viking-bones-contradict-c14-assumptions / for more information.

4. See https://www.icr.org/article/doesnt-carbon-dating-prove-earth-old and other articles from icr.org

Bible based predictions, so they keep having to manipulate and complicate the Big Bang Theory to avoid scrapping it completely.

One example of the complications and manipulations of the Big Bang Theory is dark matter. To make their mathematical equations work (mostly), they have had to create dark matter and dark energy. The majority of the matter in the universe is supposedly dark matter/energy. Nobody has seen it or sensed it. Nobody really knows what it is, but it supposedly exists. If it doesn't the math doesn't work for the Big Bang theory. It looks like dark matter is a rescuing device to save the Big Bang Theory from abject failure. It is based on nothing more than conjecture and wishing.

Many of the problems with the Big Bang Theory are complicated, so I will stick to some of the simpler points. I will especially focus on the fact that the Big Bang Theory requires many billions of years while the creation account and the genealogies in the Bible give an age of only around 6,000 years.

The Big Bang Theory says all matter exploded from a single infinitesimal point. How did we go from nothing (or everything sitting in a single point), and then when nothing happened, suddenly everything came into being? Without an outside force (God), it makes zero sense. We also can't say that God caused the Big Bang because Genesis 1 says it happened in another way.

We are told that stars formed all by themselves and are still forming (even though nobody has ever seen a star form or forming.). We are told that the gases Hydrogen and Helium coalesced to form stars. The problem with that is that everyone who has ever studied gases knows that gases expand to fill the available space. They don't coalesce closer together, especially after an explosion (Big Bang). This is 100% contradictory to known science.

Spiral galaxies spin faster in the middle than they do at the edges. Over time the spiral winds up until the spiral is not visible, yet we see lots of beautiful spiral galaxies all over that are not wound up. Based on their spin rates, they can't be billions of years old.

Comets orbit the sun in elliptical orbits. They spend most of their time in the outer reaches of our solar system, but periodically come in close to the sun where they lose lots of their mass, which is mostly ice with some dust. That is why a comet has a tail. The tail is the mass of the comet flowing away from the comet. Based on their orbital frequency (how quickly they circle/orbit the Sun) and the percentage of mass lost when the comets approach the sun, if the solar system was truly billions of years old, there should be no comets left. After a few million years, there should be no comets at all.

What have Big Bang proponents done to compensate for the comet evidence against their theory? They made up the Oort Cloud. Supposedly, so far out of the solar system that we can't sense it, there is a repository of comets. Every so often one of these comets gets knocked into orbit of the sun. What physical evidence is there of an Oort cloud? Absolutely none. They posit that it exists because, if the solar system is billions of years old, there shouldn't be any comets left, so comets have to come from somewhere, so there must be a repository so far out that we can see it or sense it in any other way. The Oort Cloud is talked about as a fact, but there actually is zero physical evidence of its existence. It is a figment of their imagination used as a rescuing device for their failed billions of years.

Earth's magnetic field is decreasing. It has a half life of about 1400 years. (meaning every 1400 years its field strength halves in power). 30,000 years ago, the electrical heating in the core would be more than a million times greater than it is today, which would destroy the planet. That strong magnetic field would also rip the iron right out of your blood. Therefore the Earth must be less than 30,000 years old.

The long age scientists have come up with a rescuing theory of a dynamo keeping the magnetic field going, but the dynamo theory doesn't match the evidence on Earth or the other planets in the solar system. The explanation is somewhat complicated, so for a detailed explanation I will refer you to <u>Earth's Mysterious Magnetism and that of other Celestial Orbs</u> by D.R. Humphreys, Ph.D. and M.J. De Spain.

The Moon moves 1.5 inches away from Earth every year (due to tides and Earth spinning faster than the Moon's rotation. The rate would've been faster when the Moon was closer to Earth.) The Moon would be touching Earth 1.4 million years ago, but secular scientists say the Earth and moon are 4 billion years old.[5] If the Earth is only about 6,000 yeas old, as the Bible describes, the Moon would only be 730 feet closer at creation roughly 6,000 years ago. This would make no difference in

---

5. One theory for the moon is that a large asteroid crashed into the Earth and the moon is a huge blob of molten Earth that was knocked into space. If evolution has a chance of being true it must have been going on for much longer than 1.4 million years and life could not have survived such a catastrophic event. If the moon is just a captured asteroid that started orbiting the Earth at some later date, then it didn't exist during most of the existence of life on Earth, but the tides are needed to keep the shallow seas healthy and conducive to life. Neither theory of the moon allows for hundreds of millions of years of life.

the interaction between the Moon and Earth or with eclipses.[6] The important tides would be the same. There would be no harmful gravitational effects from the Moon being too close. If the Earth and Moon were billions of years old, there would be catastrophic effects that would have made evolution on Earth impossible.

If you look into solar brightness, ocean salinity, continental erosion, helium in the atmosphere, radio-isotope dating errors, supernovas, soft tissue in dinosaur bones, carbon 14 in diamonds and coal, fossils, bent rocks, transcontinental sedimentation, and Niagara Falls, you can find many other evidences of a young Earth that contradict what the supposed "experts" say.

The evidence of the age of the Earth just doesn't match the Big Bang Theory or billions of years, but it is consistent with the Biblical description of the creation of the Earth and the Global Flood.

---

6. Inexplicably the moon, which is much smaller and closer, and the sun, which is so much larger and farther away, look the same size to people on Earth. This allows for a perfect eclipse, where the moon exactly blocks the sun, allowing people to look straight at the sun, and allowing people to see and study the coronasphere. There are no known planet/moon pairs where this is true other than Earth.

For much more information, you can check out https://www .icr.org/ and https://answersingenesis.org/ , which are two of the best resources I have found to strengthen your faith and prove that science supports the Bible, not refutes the Bible. Best of all, many of these resources are free. I do recommend buying some of their books and videos. They are money well spent and I have quite the collection myself.

Did Life Really Evolve from Random Chemical Reactions?

Another part of the secular "proof" against the Bible is the Theory of Evolution which states that somehow naturally oc-curring minerals and chemicals combined together to form complex cells with the most complicated code ever invented (DNA) and that this single cell somehow mutated/evolved into all of the life existing in the world. On the other hand, the Bible says plants were spoken into existence on the 3rd day of creation, that birds and water creatures were created on the 5th day of creation, and that land animals and man were created on the 6th day of creation. The Bible also says that all life was created "according to its kind."

When God says that each plant was created "after their kind with seed in them" and each animal was created "after their kind," it doesn't allow for the purported evolution from chemicals, to single celled animals, to plants, to sea creatures, to land animals, to man. Which theory best fits the evidence?

For most of the history of mankind, people thought life could spontaneously arise. Raw meat, left out, would have maggots appear in it. Flies would seemingly appear out of animal dung. Italian Physician Francesco Redi in 1668, showed that if you kept flies away from the meat that no maggots appeared. What was believed to be the spontaneous appearance of maggots and flies was actually just the life cycle of flies producing flies. After some failed experiments and some well done experiments by others, Louis Pasteur conclusively proved that spoiled food (from bacteria, fungi, etc.) was due to contamination with life and not spontaneous generation of life. Experimental Science had disproven biogenesis (life coming from non-life) and instead shown that life comes from life, not spontaneous generation.

There is only one experiment that I have found that claims to have proven that life can come from non-life, the Miller-Urey Experiment. In reality all they did was create some amino acids, which is a long way from creating life. Even for that, the experiment had massive problems and actually did a better job of proving that life cannot come from non-life.

First Stanley Miller and Harold Urey concluded that the atmosphere when life began must have been reducing rather than oxidizing because all experiments to that point had been unable to produce any pre-life compounds due to everything being oxidized. (There is no physical evidence of a low oxygen, high methane atmosphere.).

They filled a sealed glass container with methane, ammonia, and hydrogen (even though these gases are toxic to life). Then they added water vapor to simulate an ocean, heated the water to boiling, and struck the gases with 60,000 volt tungsten sparks. Because the compounds created were immediately destroyed, they added a water cooled condenser to condense the mixture, causing it to fall into a water trap that would protect the compounds created. (This doesn't sound like a likely condition on Earth, nor does any of this sound like conditions conducive to life.)

After a couple of days there was a stain in the trap. They analyzed the residue. The solids were mostly a toxic, carcinogenic mixture of organic compounds similar to what might be formed by burning tobacco. No amino acids were produced in the first attempt. On the second attempt, they managed to produce small quantities of the simplest amino acids, mostly glycine and alanine.

One problem with the experiment is that life only uses left-handed[7] organic molecules, but the Miller-Urey experiment produced an equal amount of right- and left-handed amino acids. How could proteins be formed in a mixture of right and left- handed amino acids and only use the left-handed amino acids? If even one right-handed amino acid is used, the protein has the wrong shape and won't work.

In order to make the experiment "work," they had to use a toxic atmosphere that almost certainly never existed. They had to immediately remove the compounds from this atmosphere or they would be immediately destroyed. How does this happen in the real world? It was hard enough to do in a lab. All life that we know of would be killed by this environment. For this to be proof of life, we would require that the early Earth have this toxic atmosphere, of which there is no evidence, have some way to save organic compounds from this environment until the atmosphere changed to the current atmosphere, then somehow select only the left-handed amino acids to make proteins. This doesn't even take into account the formation of the more complex amino acids or the necessary enzymes, nucle-

---

7. Left-handed and right-handed refer to how the protein is folded. A right-hand folded protein, with the exact same chemical makeup, acts differently than a left-handed folded protein and can't replace the left-handed protein in an organic system.

ic acids (precursor to DNA/RNA), carbohydrates, polymers, and other chemical compounds, then organizing them into a cell. It takes massive faith to believe this could possibly be the way life formed.

When scientists first discovered the cell, it looked like tiny rooms and seemed very simple. Now we know that even the simplest cell is more complex than the most complex factory on Earth. The information stored in the DNA, the chemical machines, and the complex organelles are so complicated that man can't fathom the details of them and keep discovering more and more complicated forms and actions. There is nothing simple about a cell and there is no evidence that it could have formed accidentally or spontaneously.

Most evolutionary scientists who have studied how life could have begun, have given up on figuring out how life could begin because it is so incomprehensibly hard. They make sure not to mention these problems when speaking to those outside their field. Often they try to push it even farther into the past and farther into space with theories that imply that life came from outer space.

Most evolutionary scientists now focus most of their time and speaking on one life form transforming into another life form. Before going into details on this, I need to explain the difference between micro-evolution (believed by all scientists) and macro-evolution.

Christian scientists used to look at evolution through the lens of the difference between micro- and macro-evolution (some still do). They considered micro-evolution as small genetic variations that cause minor changes in a life form, but do not allow a change from one kind to another kind. Macro-evolution is the theory that allows enough variation to change between kinds from one celled life all the way to man. There has never been evidence that macro-evolution has ever happened.

There is now new research being done by the Institute for Creation Research (ICR.org) showing that changes, within a kind, are more often the result of engineering design by God. God designed His creation to fulfill His mandate to fill the Earth. This required creatures to carry genetic diversity that allows trait changes that allow the creatures to survive in different environments. This actually better fits the evidence because there are no known examples of new information being created to evolve one creature into another or to give one creature a new trait. Most (if not all) genetic mutation is either neutral (cannot be selected for) or harmful. When a genetic mutation is helpful, it is almost always (if not always, I am hesitant to use absolutes) a loss of information that helps the organism survive in a particular environment (like a lab), but the loss of information makes the organism less likely to survive across multiple environments.

The overwhelming majority of genetic mutations are harmful or neutral. They happen constantly, in any individual organism. There are usually more slightly harmful mutations than helpful ones making it so any potentially beneficial mutations cannot be selected. (This is assuming non-intelligent "nature" can actually "select" for beneficial mutations. Notice how evolutionists have to personify "nature" as their own god in order to make their naturalistic theory seem to work.). In reality, if life had actually been around for hundreds of millions of years and had been mutating at near present rates, then life would have been mutated out of existence ages ago.

Instead God designed variability in the DNA of all life to allow the recombination of DNA to allow life to have the traits necessary to thrive in multiple environments. In addition, things like epigenetics, that turns genes on and off, allows changes to happen quickly to allow organisms to adjust to changes in their environment in a timely fashion. Epigenetics even allows organisms to change back when the environment changes back to the original environment. As we learn more and more about life, anyone with an open mind can discover how amazing God's design of life is. The design inherent in life is so obvious that even the die-hard evolutionists talk about the appearance of design

Chapter Review Questions:

1. Have the "experts" caused you to doubt the validity and trustworthiness of the Bible?

2. Has learning more about the science supporting the Bible helped you to trust the Bible, or at least stop denying the Bible?

3. What new information have you learned that has increased your trust of the Bible?

4. Do you have more questions that you need answered? Will you check out the mentioned references to find out more?

Chapter Five

What Should I Do About My Need?

We learned that God is an awesome and holy God who is the Creator of everything we know. We learned that we are guilty of disobeying God and of discounting His awesomeness and holiness and that we therefore deserve death. What does this mean for my life, personally?

Jesus Provided a Way:

The good news is that Jesus died for our sins to pay the debt that we owe for our many sins. There are many verses that tell about the love of God for His creation and the way to salvation from our many sins.

"For God so loved the world that He gave His one and only Son, that whoever believes in Him should not perish but have eternal life." (John 3:16).

"For there is one God and one mediator between God and mankind, the man Christ Jesus." (1 Timothy 2:5)

"We have peace with God through our Lord Jesus Christ." (Romans 5:1)

"I [Jesus] have come that they may have life, and that they may have it more abundantly." (John 10:10)

"For Christ also suffered once for sins, the righteous for the unrighteous, to bring you to God." (1 Peter 3:18)

The God and creator of the universe is so loving that He made a way for us to get right with Him when we were not able to do so ourselves. He did what we could never do. He provided a path to righteousness that we are incapable of following on our own.

The only way to be right with God is to live a perfect life with not a single sin. We can't do that. Nobody ever did until Jesus came down to Earth as a man. He lived the perfect life that we couldn't. He did what God demands and did it perfectly. He then took our sins onto Himself and paid the penalty (through His death on the cross) that God required so we don't have to pay it. He offers us His righteousness if we confess our sins and trust Him. What an amazing God and Savior we serve.

We can know that He can save us because He not only died on a cross to pay the penalty for our sins, but He also rose from the dead 3 days later. We don't serve a dead god. We serve the living God who takes away the sins of the world.

Does Everyone Go to Heaven?

Does this mean that everyone is in a right relationship with God or that everyone will be going to heaven? Unfortunately for many, but righteously, the answer is "No." He provided a way, but we must chose to take it. We must accept the gift of

God. We must confess (admit) our sins to Him, acknowledge who He is and what He did for us, and ask His forgiveness. We must put our trust in Him. He has done all of the hard work, but we must admit our faults and trust in Him.

"Yet to all who did receive Him, to those who believed in His name, He gave the right to become children of God." (John 1:12)

"If you declare with your mouth, 'Jesus is Lord,' and believe in your heart that God raised Him from the dead, you will be saved." (Romans 10:9)

"If we confess our sins, He is faithful and righteous to forgive us our sins and to cleanse us from all unrighteousness." (1 John 1:9)

He doesn't ask much of us, but we do have to actively and intentionally accept His gift. This makes sense because the greatest sin we can commit is to deny our creator God and deny all that He has done for us.

God created us to have a relationship with Him, so we will never feel complete joy and peace until we do what we were created to do. As our creator He has the right to demand that we fulfill our created function. If we choose to ignore this function, He has the right to do with us as He wishes.

"But now, O Lord, You are our Father,
We are the clay, and You our potter;
And all of us are the work of Your hand."(Isaiah 64:8)

"Or does not the potter have a right over the clay, to make from the same lump one vessel for honorable use and another for common use?" (Romans 9:21)

"For since the creation of the world His invisible attributes, His eternal power and divine nature, have been clearly seen, being understood through what has been made, so that they are without excuse."(Romans 1:20)

Don't wait until you feel ready. Don't try to get right before asking for His salvation. Don't wait to know everything. You don't know how many days you have left. You need to get right with God now. Trust Him. Ask for His forgiveness. Confess His majesty. There is nothing to lose and so much to gain.

Chapter Review Questions:

1. Can I earn my way to heaven or earn a relationship with God? (Isaiah 64:6-8)

2. Can anyone live a life pleasing to God? (Ephesians 2:8-10)

3. What did Jesus do for us? (Colossians 1:15-23)

4. How does Jesus's death and resurrection affect my relationship with God? (Romans 4:6-11)

5. How does my faith in Jesus's death change me? (Philippians 3:7-16)

Chapter Six

What Should I Do If I Already Know Jesus as Savior?

Many readers may already know Jesus as savior, but they may not have given God the thanks, praise, and reverence that He deserves. So many of us have been told that God loves us, but not told that He is a holy God. So many of us have been told what not to do, but maybe not what God wants us to do. So many of us have a history of treating God as a buddy or a magic genie who fulfills wishes. Instead we need to honor and obey God as He commands and deserves.

Ephesians chapter 5 is a good place to go to discover what God really wants from us.

"Therefore be imitators of God, as beloved children." (Ephesians 5:1) God wants us to imitate Jesus. He wants us to do what He does and not do what He doesn't do, and to love others as He did and still does.

"And walk in love, as Christ loved us and gave Himself up for us, a fragrant offering and sacrifice to God." (Ephesians 5:2) We are to love God and love others as Jesus loves God and loves us. When Jesus was asked by the Pharisees what the greatest commandment was, He replied, *"You shall love the Lord your God with all your heart and with all your soul and with all your mind. [38]This is the great and first commandment. [39]And a second is like it: You shall love your neighbor as yourself. [40]On these two commandments depend all the Law and the Prophets."* (Matthew 22:37-40) Nothing is more important than acting in love towards others. All that we do should be influenced by love. Most importantly, Biblical love is an action, not just a feeling.

"[3]But sexual immorality and all impurity or covetousness must not even be named among you, as is proper among saints. [4]Let there be no filthiness nor foolish talk nor crude joking, which are out of place, but instead let there be thanksgiving. [5]For you may be sure of this, that everyone who is sexually immoral or impure, or who is covetous (that is, an idolater), has no inheritance in the kingdom of Christ

and God." (Ephesians 5:3-5) Our lives should look different than the world. One of the ways we can be most distinct is by separating ourselves from the sexual sins and crude joking that is so common in the world. We need to be thankful for all things and not covetous (wanting what others have). Unsaved people are almost always defined by their desire for what they can't have and their ungratefulness for what they do have. Christians should be thankful in all circumstances knowing that *"...we know that God causes all things to work together for good to those who love God, to those who are called according to His purpose."* (Romans 8:28). When we are thankful even in difficult circumstances, people see the difference in us and God is honored.

"[6]Let no one deceive you with empty words, for because of these things the wrath of God comes upon the sons of disobedience. [7]Therefore do not become partners with them; [8]for at one time you were darkness, but now you are light in the Lord. Walk as children of light [9](for the fruit of light is found in all that is good and right and true), [10]and try to discern what is pleasing to the Lord." (Ephesians 5:6-10) God does not want us to be in the likeness of the world or the world's wisdom, but in the likeness of Jesus and in accordance with the Bible. If we do not want to be deceived, we need to read, study, and know the Bible. We want

to memorize scripture so we have God's word with us always when we need it. *"These things I have spoken to you, so that in Me you may have peace. In the world you have tribulation, but take courage; I have overcome the world."* (John 16:33)

> *"11 Take no part in the unfruitful works of darkness, but instead expose them. 12For it is shameful even to speak of the things that they do in secret. 13But when anything is exposed by the light, it becomes visible, 14for anything that becomes visible is light. Therefore it says,*
> *"Awake, O sleeper,*
> *and arise from the dead,*
> *and Christ will shine on you."* (Ephesians 5:11-14)

Not only are we supposed to believe in the truth, but we are supposed to stand for the truth. When lies are spoken, we are to speak up in a loving manner. We are told *"But in your hearts revere Christ as Lord. Always be prepared to give an answer to everyone who asks you to give the reason for the hope that you have. But do this with gentleness and respect."* (1 Peter 3:15) It is important that our response is done *"with gentleness and respect"* rather than to win the argument. Remember that we have God on our side and He is truth. We shouldn't be hesitant or afraid to speak the truth. Truth and love, not popularity, should be our motivation when we speak against the lies of the world. We always want to speak the truth, but we want to use it as a tool to help lead sinners to life in Christ and not as a club to bludgeon them to death.

"15 Look carefully then how you walk, not as unwise but as wise, 16making the best use of the time, because the days are evil. 17Therefore do not be foolish, but understand what the will of the Lord is." (Ephesians 5:15-17) Wisdom is more than knowledge. We need knowledge to be wise, but we also need the help of the Holy Spirit to wisely interpret our knowledge. Wisdom is also more than head knowledge. If we don't act on that knowledge, it isn't true wisdom. The more evil the actions of those around us, the more wisdom we need and the more necessary it is to act on that wisdom. Without trusting in Jesus, relying on the Holy Spirit, and continual prayer, we cannot truly be wise.

"18And do not get drunk with wine, for that is dissipation, but be filled with the Spirit," (Ephesians 5:18) When most people look at this verse, the focus on the first half about not getting drunk. It is true that it is unwise to be drunk because

it leads to unwise thoughts and actions. I do not believe, however, that this is the main point of this verse. When a person has a small glass of wine with dinner, the wine has very little effect on the person. It usually has no noticeable effect on their speech or actions. If a person drinks a whole bottle of wine on an empty stomach, however, their thoughts, speech, and actions are modified and it is obvious the person is drunk and has been drinking. In comparison, a person who is saved has the Holy Spirit, but a person who is filled with the Spirit will have their thoughts, speech, and actions affected. *"Now when they saw the boldness of Peter and John, and perceived that they were uneducated, common men, they were astonished. And they recognized that they had been with Jesus."* (Acts 4:13) We need to be so filled with the Holy Spirit that when people interact with us, they see Jesus in us. We want everyone who meets us to *"recognized that they (we) had been with Jesus."*

"19... speaking to one another in psalms and hymns and spiritual songs, singing and making melody with your heart to the Lord;" (Ephesians 5:19) One of the purposes of people is to worship God. This can be singing at church, singing while we are living our lives, praising in prayer, or publicly speaking of God's utter awesomeness. It can even be just acknowledging His greatness in our hearts. We need to make

sure we understand what a truly awesome God we serve and act accordingly. Our speech should also differentiate us from nonbelievers. We should speak good and useful words and not crass and harmful words.

"20... always giving thanks for all things in the name of our Lord Jesus Christ to God, even the Father." (Ephesians 5:20) Thanks needs to be a part of everything we do. We need to thank God for His creation. We need to thank God for how He provides for us. We need to thank God for how He saved us. We even need to thank God for the hardship we experience knowing that it is for good and according to His purpose. Even hardship can be used to grow our faith, help us draw closer to God, help us to rely on God, and help us to minister to others. In every thing that happens to us, there is good that comes from it if we look hard enough. God is in control and everything that happens, happens for a purpose. Sometimes we may not know His purpose until eternity, but we can trust that He is working for good. *"And we know that God causes **all** things to work together for good to those who love God, to those who are called according to His purpose."* (Romans 8:28) We need to remember that being thankful is not just a feeling; it is a choice.

"21... and be subject to one another in the fear of Christ." (Ephesians 5:21) Possibly the most difficult command given

to us is to submit. God talks about us submitting to Him, but also submitting to government, employers, husbands, parents, etc. Yes, there are occasions where we must chose submitting to God rather than man, but we must be careful. None of us like submitting to someone with whom we disagree. It is easy to justify to ourselves that our actions are submitting to God when we are just putting our will first. There are numerous passages in the Bible telling His people to submit, such as *"Remind them to be subject to rulers, to authorities, to be obedient, to be ready for every good deed."* (Titus 3:1)   By submitting we are definitely making ourselves look different than the world. "39But I say to you, do not resist an evil person; but whoever slaps you on your right cheek, turn the other to him also. 40If anyone wants to sue you and take your shirt, let him have your coat also. 41Whoever forces you to go one mile, go with him two. 42Give to him who asks of you, and do not turn away from him who wants to borrow from you." (Matthew 5:39-42) This is not easy, but the Holy Spirit will aid us in obeying His will. Ultimately we need to submit to God before all others, but God has commanded us to submit to other authorities, in humility, except when the other authority directly contradicts God's word.

The rest of Ephesians 5 details some of the ways we are to submit and to love. I don't believe I need to explain this clear passage, but I'll include it in order to be complete.

> *"*^{25}*Husbands, love your wives, just as Christ also loved the church and gave Himself up for her,* ^{26}*so that He might sanctify her, having cleansed her by the washing of water with the word,* ^{27}*that He might present to Himself the church in all her glory, having no spot or wrinkle or any such thing; but that she would be holy and blameless.* ^{28}*So husbands ought also to love their own wives as their own bodies. He who loves his own wife loves himself;* ^{29}*for no one ever hated his own flesh, but nourishes and cherishes it, just as Christ also does the church,* ^{30}*because we are members of His body.* ^{31}*For this reason a man shall leave his father and mother and shall be joined to his wife, and the two shall become one flesh.* ^{32}*This mystery is great; but I am speaking with reference to Christ and the church.* ^{33}*Nevertheless, each individual among you also is to love his own wife even as himself, and the wife must see to it that she respects her husband."* (Ephesians 5:25-33)

This only touches on what we need to do to properly serve our Savior and Creator. We need to read our Bible daily, pray continually, fellowship with other believers, go to Church, and share what we have learned with others, believers and non-believers.

I hope you will trust Jesus and seek to serve Him faithfully so that people will see you and know that you belong to Jesus.

Chapter Review Questions:

1. Who should be the model for our behavior? (Hebrews 13:7-14) (2 Thessalonians 3:6-13)

2. How am I guilty of immoral actions? Immoral thoughts? (Matthew 5:27-28) Watching inappropriate movies or listening to inappropriate music? Other ways?

3. What is the difference between knowledge and wisdom? What can I do to grow in wisdom? (James 1:5) (Proverbs 1:7)

4. How can I be more loving? To whom do I need to show more love? (Luke 6:27-36)

5. How can I be filled with the Holy Spirit? What does

this mean? (Acts 4:27-31)

6. How have I misused my speech? What changes should I make to my speech? (James 3:1-10)

7. What do I need to be thankful for? What difficult/unpleasant thing should I be thankful for? (1 Thessalonians 5:16-22) (Psalm 111)

8. To whom do I need to submit? (Colossians 3:18-25)

For more by this author and to get updates on future books check out:

https://trustjesus.substack.com/

Acknowledgements

I wanted to thank the various people who helped make this book a reality. I am grateful to Charlene Bichel, Harry Guess, and Donna Koslowsky, who read my drafts and gave me feedback and encouragement. I am thankful to Darcie Gudger, my fellow author, who helped me through the process of turning my manuscript into the final product and answered all of the questions I had on how to make this book a reality. I especially want to thank my son, Joshua, and my husband, Kendell, who spent lots of time acting as my editors fixing errors in clarity and grammar, and especially helping me get my commas right, my punctuation inside quotation marks, and capitalizing all references to God. This work wouldn't be what it is without their help.

Most of all I want to thank my God and my Savior, who took away my sins and who inspired me to write. I never planned to be a writer; I never wanted to be a writer, but God inspired me to write. I had to submit to His calling. Now I can't stop writing. I hope this book has been an inspiration to you and will help you to grow closer to our awesome God, Creator, and Savior.

For more by this author and to get updates on future books check out:

https://trustjesus.substack.com/